Making Rules

by Vickey Herold

Table of Contents

I need to know these words.

adult

community

laws

responsibility

rules

CLASSROOM RULES
1 Be respectful of others
2 Come to class prepared
3 Remain in seat at all times
(unless otherwise directed)

vote

Why Are Rules Important at Home?

Rules can make life better for a family. Some rules keep everyone in the family safe. Do you fall over toys? Do you stumble over shoes? Some people have rules about putting things away. These rules make homes safe.

▲ Rules about putting things away make a home safe.

Many rules keep the children in a family safe. Only let people that you know into your home. Ask an **adult** you trust before you open the door.

▲ Only let people that you trust come into your home.

A rule can be about **responsibility**. A responsibility is something you should do. Do you have responsibilities at home? Do you feed a pet? Does your family have rules about responsibilities?

▲ Some families share responsibilities.

Rules are often about how to behave, too. These rules help the people in a family get along. The rules are about doing what is right.

▲ Rules can be about how to behave.

Why Are Rules Important at School?

Schools also have rules about how to behave. Does your school have rules about running? Does your school have rules in the cafeteria? Think about the rules. Your school is clean and safe because of rules.

▲ Schools have rules about how to behave.

Schools have rules to keep everyone safe. Some rules are about playing safely. Does your school have rules for the playground? Does your school have rules for the gym? How do these rules keep you safe?

▲ Schools have rules to keep people safe.

Most classrooms have rules, too. Some rules are about doing the best you can. Some rules are about working well together. Rules about working well together help everyone learn. What rules does your classroom have?

CLASSROOM RULES
1 Be respectful of others
2 Come to class prepared
3 Remain in seat at all times (unless otherwise directed)

▲ **Most classrooms have rules.**

People at school often play sports. Every sport has rules. Baseball has rules. Soccer has rules. Rules keep games fair for everyone. Rules help people know how to play games.

▲ Rules keep sports fair.

Why Does a Community Need Rules?

A **community** needs rules. Rules help people live and work together. **Laws** are the rules that people in a community must follow. Every community has laws. Towns and cities have laws. Countries have laws, too.

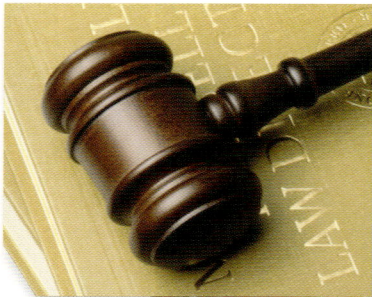

▲ Laws are rules for a community.

Laws keep people safe. Traffic laws keep people safe. People who drive must follow traffic laws.

▲ Traffic laws help people drive safely.

Communities have laws about how to behave. These laws stop people from hurting one another. The laws stop people from doing bad things.

▲ People cannot take things that belong to others.

Laws are rules that the people in a community must follow. Many communities have laws about parks. Many people follow laws about schools, too. What laws does your community have?

KEEP DOGS ON LEAD
1 MAY – 30 SEPT

▲ Every community has laws.

Who Makes the Rules?

People in charge make some rules. Adults are people in charge. Adults can make rules at home.

▲ Families have rules at home.

Principals are people in charge. Teachers are people in charge. Principals and teachers can make rules at school.

▲ Teachers make rules at school.

Groups of people can make rules, too. Does your family make rules together? Do you help make rules at school? Do you **vote** when you make the rules?

▲ People can vote to make rules.

People in communities make laws together. People vote to make laws. Voting is an important responsibility in a community.

▲ A community can vote to make laws.

Glossary

adult (uh-DULT):
a fully grown person
See page 5.

community
(kuh-MYOO-nuh-tee):
a place where people
live, work, and play
See page 12.

laws (LAWZ): rules
that people in a
community must obey
See page 12.

responsibility
(rih-spahn-suh-BIH-luh-
tee): a task someone
should do
See page 6.

rules (ROOLZ): guides
for what must happen
See page 4.

vote (VOTE):
to choose
See page 18.

Index